W9-CUW-806

THE
BLACK
PANTHER

BY
SHELLEY SWANSON SATEREN

EDITED BY
JULIE BACH

CRESTWOOD HOUSE
New York

LIBRARY OF CONGRESS CATALOGING IN PUBLICATION DATA

Sateren, Shelley Swanson.
  The black panther

  (Wildlife, habits & habitat)
  Includes index.
  SUMMARY: Describes the physical characteristics, behavior, and habitat of the black panther, the dark phase of the spotted leopard species.
  1. Leopard—Juvenile literature. [1. Leopard.] I. Title. II. Series.
QL737.C23S27   1990   599.74'428—dc20   89-28267
ISBN 0-89686-519-3

PHOTO CREDITS:

Cover: Berg & Associates: Kenneth W. Fink
Berg & Associates: (Wardene Weisser) 4, 7, 12, 15, 23, 41, 44; (Mary Van Nostrand) 10, 27, 31, 32-33; (Kenneth W. Fink) 11, 13, 20, 36-37; (Jean S. Buldain) 17; (Bob West) 18; (Nadine Orabona) 26, 28-29
David Scheel: 35

Macmillan Publishing Company
866 Third Avenue
New York, NY 10022
CRESTWOOD HOUSE Collier Macmillan Canada, Inc.

Printed in the United States of America
First Edition
10 9 8 7 6 5 4 3 2 1

TABLE OF CONTENTS

With its dark spots on dark fur, the jaguar, like the black panther, blends into its surroundings.

INTRODUCTION:

Deep in the shadows of the Asian jungle, the black panther hunts. Glancing up, this big cat searches for monkeys in the trees. Its dark coat blends with the shadows of the thick *rain forest* jungle. This dark coat acts as *camouflage*. It hides the panther from the animals it hunts.

This glossy animal with emerald green eyes slinks on. It drifts along a streamed, past a water hole. For a moment, the black panther is bathed in a small patch of sunlight. In this bright light, black spots can be seen on the black panther's dark brown coat.

Around the world, *panther* is another name for the leopard. A black panther is in fact a spotted leopard. A leopard is a *species* of animal. *Black panther* is a name given to the black *phase* of the spotted leopard species. A phase is a trait that sets some individuals of a group apart from the rest.

Black or fair, these spotted cats are all in the same species. Some are even brothers and sisters. A light-colored female may give birth to either light cubs or dark cubs. Both color cubs may be born in the same *litter*. The difference between a fair and a black cub is only a matter of color. A dark-haired human being may have a blond brother or sister. The same goes for spotted leopards.

For many years, the black panther was thought to be a species apart from the spotted leopard. But scientists know better today.

CHAPTER ONE:

A *naturalist* is a person who studies nature. He or she looks closely at plant or animal life. Some naturalists in the 1800s studied spotted leopards. They saw that the black panther was often more stocky than its light-colored cousins. They thought this unique panther should have its own name, so they called the black panther *Felis melas*. *Felis melas* means black cat in Latin.

Other naturalists believed that the black panther was nothing more than a spotted leopard with a very dark coat. Soon their belief would be proven correct.

The scientists agree

By the 1930s, scientists had learned that light and dark spotted leopards belonged to the same species. They watched light-colored female leopards closely. Sometimes a female bore a black cub along with two or three fair cubs. This proved that black and fair cubs were the same species. The black cub would grow into a black panther, but it was a spotted leopard just the same.

The scientists learned that black cubs are *melanistic*. Their skins and hair are dark as a result of high amounts of *pigment*. There is pigment in human skin and animal fur. It turns the skin or fur shades of brown. Melanistic cases are common in all cats. They are very common among leopards.

The melanistic trait is a result of *heredity*. Heredity is the transfer of traits from parents to children. Parents pass on traits such as hair and eye color to their children.

6

A melanistic, or black, jaguar and the more common fair-furred cat.

Certain cells inside the human body contain thousands of *genes*. A gene is like a tiny computer, filled with information. Genes determine which traits parents pass on to their children.

The spotted leopard also has genes. Two genes work together to decide the coat color of a cub. Each cub receives two coat-color genes. One comes from the father.

SPOTTED LEOPARD

BLACK PANTHER

The other comes from the mother. If a cub gets two light-coat genes from its parents, the cub will be light. If a cub gets two black-coat genes, it will be black. But if a cub gets one light-coat gene and one black-coat gene, it will be light. This is because the spotted leopard's *dominant gene* is the gene for a light coat. The light-coat gene is dominant over the black-coat gene. A dominant gene has the

8

final say in passing on a trait. This is why some spotted leopard litters have two or three fair cubs and only one black cub.

Scientists today agree that color is the main difference between a spotted leopard and a black panther. Black panthers are simply spotted leopards that have very dark brown hair.

A broad name

In parts of the world today, the term *panther* is used broadly. In India, all leopards, black or fair, are called panthers. In parts of North and South America, jaguars, pumas, and cougars are called panthers. Sometimes black jaguars are called black panthers. But the most common use of the word *panther* today refers to the spotted leopard species that lives in Asia and Africa.

In this book, the name *black panther* refers only to the black phase of the spotted leopard species. Black panthers along with their light-colored sisters, brothers, and cousins are called spotted leopards.

A vast range

The spotted leopard has a wider *range,* or is found in more places, than any of the other big cats. These cats roam deserts, rain forests, and rocky mountains.

These dark and light colored jaguar cubs playing with their mother came from the same litter.

It is no wonder that members of the spotted leopard species vary. They live in all kinds of climates and conditions. Coat lengths and shades may differ. The sizes of the cats and their spots also may differ.

A spotted leopard's coat can vary from a dull straw color to a rich tigerlike red. Or it might be a chestnut color or a deep brown. In the humid, rainy tropics of Asia, the spotted leopard's coat is often darker. As we have seen, the darkest cats are called panthers. In hot, dry regions of Africa, the coats are lighter. Light colors reflect sunlight and heat. They keep the animals cool.

In hot desert regions, spotted leopards' bodies are often slender. A slender build is better at getting rid of body heat. And in hot deserts or tropics, spotted leopards have short fur to keep cool. Those in cool climates have thicker fur to keep warm.

Members of the spotted leopard species, both black and fair, differ in size. The average adult male is eight feet long from his nose to the end of his tail. Normal tail length is two to three feet. Most adult females weigh 75 to

This spotted leopard is a true panther. It is stronger and quieter than other cats in its family and has distinctive spots.

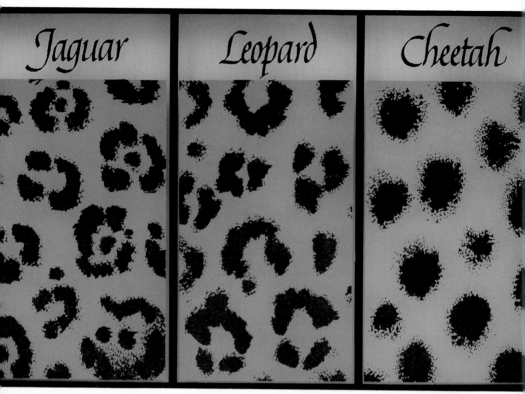

The spots on jaguars, leopards, and cheetahs are different shapes. The rosettes on the leopard look like paw prints.

100 pounds. Adult males weigh more. The average adult stands two feet high at the shoulder. Females are about a foot shorter in length than males.

Spotted leopards are covered with *rosettes*. Rosettes are dark brown, almost black, spots. Each rosette is made up of five small dots that form a circle. They look very much like animal paw prints. On a fair spotted leopard, the center of each rosette is darker than the cat's light background color. The black panther's rosettes are visible only in bright light.

Many people find the black panther the most interesting of all spotted leopards, because it is rarer and more unusual than its fair cousins. But whether black, tan, straw colored or chestnut colored, all members of the spotted leopard species are handsome. If the lion is the king of beasts, then the spotted leopard is the prince. For its size, it is the strongest and bravest of the big cats.

A close look at the rosettes on a live leopard.

CHAPTER TWO:

Members of the spotted leopard species, including the black panther, are great hunters. They are the most athletic of the big cats. They have a unique food storage system and are not fussy about their diets. This chapter examines some of the traits that the black panther has in common with its light-colored relatives.

An invisible hunter

During the day, the black panther lies hidden under thick plants or shrubs. It may sleep there or high in a tree, draped over a branch. Most black panthers hunt in the early morning or at night. In regions where there are many humans, black panthers are all *nocturnal*. They sleep during the day and hunt at night.

The black panther is silent and cautious. Its padded paws are soft and quiet. The hair on its legs absorbs noise. This cat can seem to disappear in a moment by freezing itself. It sits perfectly still and blends in with the jungle background. It becomes invisible to its enemies. More importantly, the black panther cannot be seen by its *prey*, the animal it hunts. Because the black panther is so quiet and hard to see, it is known as "the ghost of the forest."

Silent and sleek, the black panther is known as the ghost of the forest.

At dusk, the black panther slinks into a bush or some other cover in the middle of a large grazing area. Here, game animals gather during the dark hours. The cat waits in this spot, night after night. It waits patiently until an animal passes close enough for the panther to strike.

When the black panther hunts, it is a stalker, not a runner. It walks slowly and creeps very close to its prey.

15

Sometimes this stalking takes hours. The black panther does not waste its energy on running. It is not like the cheetah, which chases its prey.

The black panther might use a branch on a leafy tree as an *ambush*. It waits until an animal passes below. Then it pounces down onto its victim in a surprise attack.

First-rate athlete

The black panther excels in jumping and tree climbing. Though this black cat has short legs, its leaps are astounding. It can jump 25 feet and as high in the air as 12 feet.

For its size, the black panther is very powerful. It often grabs prey that is larger and weighs more than itself. For this reason, the black panther's neck and shoulder muscles are massive.

When it hunts, eighteen claws snap like jackknives out of this cat's padded paws. There are five on each front paw and four on each back paw. The panther's eyesight and night vision are sharp. Its senses of smell and hearing are keener yet. A black panther can hear the click of a camera from 20 yards away.

The black panther's long tail balances the cat when it leaps or stalks. The animal can perform great balancing acts by using its tail. One of these big cats once sprang and landed on a gatepost. Its tail moved constantly, keep-

16   *A leopard in the National Reserve in Kenya, Africa, drapes itself across the limb of a tree.*

ing it steady on the tiny perch. This would be like a house cat trying to stand on top of a broomstick.

Stashing prey in trees

After a kill, the black panther eats its fill. But if it cannot finish eating its prey, the black panther will save the

Now the fork of this tree serves as a hammock for the African panther. Later, the cat will use it as a place to stash prey.

remains, or *carcass*. It hides the carcass in the fork of a tree. The cat will return to the stash and eat it later. Prey stashed in a tree is a sure sign that a member of the spotted leopard species is near.

Up in the tree, the carcass is safe from other hungry animals. Jackals and hyenas cannot reach it. Vultures will not touch it. If the carcass was left on the ground, these birds would gobble it in a flash. Nobody knows why a black panther's kill stashed in a tree is safe from vultures.

The black panther uses its powerful leg, neck, and jaw muscles to carry a kill up into a tree. The cat braces itself on the tree trunk with the kill in its jaws. Then it slowly hoists the kill upward. The cat changes its grip inch by inch. At last it drapes its heavy cargo over a branch.

A black panther's prey often weighs as much as the panther itself, sometimes more. A South African hunter once found a 200-pound giraffe calf carcass in a tree. This carcass was draped over a branch 12 feet off the ground! Since it happened in southern Africa, where black panthers are rare, a fair spotted leopard most likely performed this feat. But a black panther is just as capable of such strength.

Not a fussy eater

The black panther is a sloppy eater. The animal uses its rough tongue to remove hair and skin from a kill. It gulps down the meat and leaves the grinding to its strong stomach.

After the cat eats its messy meal, it spends hours scrubbing itself. It washes until it is free of scent. That way other animals cannot smell the black panther. Then the cat can get close enough to another prey to catch its next meal.

The black panther spends hours scrubbing itself, but not because it likes being clean. When it is odorless, it can sneak closer to its prey without being detected.

The black panther is not fussy about its menu. It has a wide range of prey. This *carnivore* eats anything alive if it is not too big to be tackled. It might feed on deer, monkeys, or bushpigs. Or it might prey on warthogs, birds, or baboons. Some black panthers will even eat fish, frogs, mice, lizards, beetles, and sweet fruits.

Dog is a frequent food of the black panther. Black panthers have been known to charge into villages and seize pet dogs. They are easy prey for this cat since they are small and tend to wander. A dog walking alone down a dirt path is an easy catch for a big cat.

Black panthers can go for a long time without food or water if they have to. This might happen during a drought or a food shortage. Black panthers know how to adapt to hard times. They replace one kind of prey with another. If wild game is scarce, they hunt tame animals. They grab dogs, cattle, or sheep from farms. If both wild game and farm stock are scarce, the black panther may feed on human flesh. An animal that makes a habit of this is called a *man-eater.*

A wounded or ill black panther also might become a man-eater. It may have broken teeth, or its back, neck, or legs may be damaged. It might have a porcupine quill lodged in its body. Or perhaps a human hunter has shot it with a bullet. A wounded black panther needs weak prey to feed on. Humans, like dogs, are easy to catch. Humans are not born with claws, quills, or fangs for protection. Without man-made weapons, humans cannot protect themselves from black panthers that attack.

Most healthy black panthers avoid humans as long as there is enough food. There are fewer man-eating spotted leopards than man-eating lions or tigers. The normal, healthy black panther vanishes at the sight and sound of humans.

Black panthers also scavenge to get meals. A *scavenger* feeds on other animals' leftovers. It will eat any carcass lying on the ground, no matter how rotten. Black panthers are not scavengers as often as hyenas are. But at times they will find meals this way. As a result, black panthers are often poisoned. Farmers put out poisoned meat to kill wild animals when their livestock are threatened. Many spotted leopards have died from poison. This is one reason why the spotted leopard is *endangered*.

Set on survival

The black panther, like all members of its species, has no greater enemy in nature than the human. A few other enemies can cause the black panther harm. The lion, tiger, crocodile, and python are some. Packs of wild dogs or baboons can destroy this cat. Diseases and *parasites* can, too. A parasite might be a flea, tick, or worm that lives on or in the black panther. But of these few enemies, the most serious over time has been the human.

The black panther's cautious nature helps protect it against its foes. It avoids groups of wild game, knowing a pack could kill it. It safely stalks weak animals that stray from their groups. The black panther avoids open spaces and, by freezing, remains hidden from its foes.

This black cat seems able to protect itself from humans, too. It won't return to a kill if it senses the presence of a hunter. Before returning, it hides in a bush and waits. It watches and listens for hours. It will approach the kill only when it decides the place is safe from hunters.

Black panthers like this Chinese leopard can wait in ambush for hours.

Hunters often wait at a kill for a black panther to return. But this only seems to make the black panther more quiet, still, and invisible. Even when wounded, the cat stays silent. A wounded tiger groans loudly, giving away its hiding place to the hunter. But a wounded black panther doesn't made a sound. It stays hidden, suffering in silence, determined to survive.

This cautious nature has helped some black panthers survive. Fewer spotted leopards, black or fair, are shot than tigers. When this cat's enemies leave it alone, it can live 16 to 20 years in the wild.

CHAPTER THREE:

The adult black panther, like all adult spotted leopards, leads an independent life. By choice, this quiet animal lives by itself. If it sees another black panther, it turns away. Only at mating time does it look for another of its kind, and then only briefly. Occasionally one black panther wanders into another black panther's area. Moments like these are tense and can lead to fights. Fights can also happen between males during breeding seasons.

A black panther marks its area with urine and defends it by fighting. The average size of a black panther's territory is seven to ten square miles. When food is ample, this big cat might stay by itself in one area for years.

A brief romance

The black panther, like all spotted leopards, lives alone guarding its range. At times it makes a loud rasping noise. The noise sounds like a saw going back and forth on a log of wood. This noise may mean many things. It may announce a black panther's presence. It may tell other black panthers to stay off its range.

This sawing noise is also a mating call. A female makes sawing noises to attract a male. She acts playful, rolls about, and makes circles around him. The male, in turn, acts bored. He seems to want to be left alone, as usual.

As soon as mating is over, the male goes on his way. It is rare for the male and female to stay together more than a day or two. The male will take no part in raising the family. Perhaps in some cases this is best, since males in this species sometimes eat their cubs.

Growing up

After 90 to 100 days, one to six cubs are born. The cubs are furry at birth and weigh only 15 to 20 ounces. They are born blind. The tiny cats open their eyes after one to two weeks.

A female black panther, like most females of this species, bears her cubs alone. And she raises them alone. A home for her family may be a mountain cave or a space

Sensing danger, a black jaguar spits and hisses to protect her offspring.

under thick plant growth. It may be a tree trunk hollowed by fire or wood-eating insects.

The female cat is an excellent mother. She will feed and protect her cubs at all costs. The mother keeps her cubs hidden until they start to follow her, at about six to eight weeks of age.

When the mother senses danger, she hisses and spits to bring the little ones to heel. Yet, in spite of her careful

26

eyes, she cannot always prevent harm. Lions and hyenas kill spotted leopard cubs for meals. Cubs climb high in trees to escape these *predators*. This climbing skill sets the spotted leopard species apart from other big cats. Cubs excel at this talent at an early age. Still, many of them fall prey to hungry lions and hyenas.

Disease and fever can also kill the cubs. In each litter, it is rare for more than one or two cubs to live to maturity.

A jaguar tidies her cub.

A black panther cub snuggles up to its mother at the Los Angeles Zoo.

The cubs learn through play. They pounce on everything that moves. They gently attack crickets, dry leaves, and their mother's tail. Bold and bumbling, these cubs roughhouse and behave much like house-cat kittens.

On their own

Very young black panther cubs, like all young spotted leopards, have a simple menu. They eat a liquid diet of only their mothers' milk. When they are a little older, they begin to eat raw meat. The mother eats the meat herself and partly digests it. Then she vomits it up for her cubs to feed on.

Later, the cubs are able to digest meat themselves. The mother brings home small kills for them to eat. As time passes, she brings home larger prey. At last, the mother takes her cubs to the field. She begins to teach them hunting skills. A cub can make a kill on its own before it is a year old. Spotted leopard cubs, black and fair, seem to have better hunting skills than do young lions or cheetahs.

Most of these spotted cats are social only when they are growing up as cubs. Even then, their independent natures are obvious. Brothers and sisters find it hard to eat together. They fight over food. They fight until their stomachs begin to feel full. Only then do they share.

When the cubs are one to two years old, the mother sends them on their way. A male cub moves on and settles

Young cubs feed only on their mothers' milk. Here a Brazilian jaguar cub nurses until it is full.

elsewhere. He creates a territory of his own. A female cub may do the same, or she may take over part of her mother's range. It is time for the mother to mate again and raise a new batch of cubs.

When they are between one and two years old, young panthers venture out on their own.

CHAPTER FOUR:

An endangered animal exists in small numbers. Members of the spotted leopard species are able to adapt to changes in what they eat and where they live. This has helped them survive. But not many of these beautiful animals are left.

The number of spotted leopards has dropped over the years. The light-colored members have been hit the hardest, because their coats are valuable to the fur trade. But the number of black panthers has dropped, too.

The most dangerous enemy

For decades, the spotted leopard has been disturbed by humans. Farmers have killed it with poison and traps. Hunters have killed it for adventure. The fashion trade has made coats out of its fur.

Sometimes when farmers kill spotted leopards to protect their livestock, a worse thing happens. Normally, these big cats help keep wild pig and baboon numbers low. When spotted leopards are killed off, the number of pigs and baboons increases. These wild creatures can do more harm to farms and livestock than spotted leopards can.

Hunting has also endangered these big cats. Humans kill spotted leopards that are man-eaters. And they continue to hunt them for sport. Hunting a spotted leopard is thought to be more exciting than hunting a tiger because the spotted leopard can hide so well and is hard to track.

People on safari view a curious leopard from the safety of a Jeep.

Fashionable spots

The fashion market has caused great damage to this species. The leopard's coat is highly prized in the fur trades. Spotted coats are very stylish.

Plush fur jackets were once high fashion. Unfortunately, it took the deaths of five to seven cats to make one coat.

In the 1940s and 1950s, spotted fur coats appeared on the market. In the 1960s and early 1970s, spotted leopard coats became very popular in Europe and the United States. European and North American hunting companies ruled the trade. They trapped most of the spotted leopards in Africa. A woman's spotted leopard coat required five to seven skins. One coat could cost thousands

of dollars. This money-making scheme meant that vast numbers of spotted leopards were destroyed.

On June 2, 1970, the spotted leopard was added to the United States's endangered species list. In this country, the spotted leopard could no longer be imported or exported to make money. Still, Americans brought spotted leopard coats home from Europe. American hunters, too, were allowed to bring their skins to the United States.

On July 1, 1975, 34 countries signed a treaty. These countries, including the United States, agreed not to import or export any endangered animal skins. Today, over 100 countries have signed this treaty.

Spotted leopard skins are no longer legally sold in the United States. But spotted leopard skins are still sold in parts of Europe and Asia. Most of these animals are killed in Asia. Some of the trade is legal and some is illegal. *Poachers*, people who hunt illegally, continue to break the treaty that tries to protect the spotted leopard. Great damage has been done to this species by the fur trade.

Luckily, the fur trade has spared the black panther. Its spots are not as visible, so its dark coat is not in such demand.

CHAPTER FIVE:

The black panther is the darkest of all the spotted leopards. Black panthers are common in jungle regions of India and southeast Asia. Melanistic spotted leopards occur most often in areas such as these. This is also true in the jaguar family. More black jaguars are born in the Amazon jungle than elsewhere in Central and South America. Scientists do not know why melanistic big cats occur more often in tropical jungles than in other areas.

Jungle dwellers

Black panthers are common in hot, steaming tropical rain forests. They are common in Java and Malaysia in the Indian Ocean. In Malaysia, as many as half the spotted leopards are believed to be black. Of course, a black cub can turn up in almost any litter anywhere. But, in fact, few are born in Africa. People have spotted black panthers in dry, rocky country, but this is rare.

Scientists suggest that the very dark coat camouflages the black panther. It makes the cat hard to see in the shadowy gloom of the tropics. This may help explain the high survival rate of black panthers in the tropics. But this is still just a theory.

One thing is certain: Thick forests like those in Malaysia protect animals from humans. It is hard for humans to hunt in these forests. This has helped save many black panthers, as well as their light-colored relatives.

Black panther families

Black panthers are often larger in size than their fair-furred cousins. The diet of game is richer in the jungle regions where black panthers live.

Black panthers may also have stronger family ties than do their cousins from hotter, drier climates. In parts of Asia, groups of black cats have been seen eating the same kill. Where food is plentiful, the male panther tends to stay with the family. Panthers do not need to defend private ranges in areas rich with game.

Spooky ghost stories

For hundreds of years, people have found black cats frightening. Perhaps you have feared a black cat crossing your path. You are not alone. These fears are ages old. In the Middle Ages, a black cat was even thought to be the devil.

Myths like these surround the black panther, too. Movies, books, and adventure magazines continue these myths. The writers often describe the black panther as dangerous and make it look like a wicked superleopard.

But these are just tales. The black panther's dark color does not make it stronger or more dangerous than other cats. Its body is often larger because of its better diet in the tropics. This means it can kill larger prey. But that is all. The belief that the black panther is more savage is just a myth.

Because of their supernatural stealth, black panthers have been the subject of several scary stories and movies.

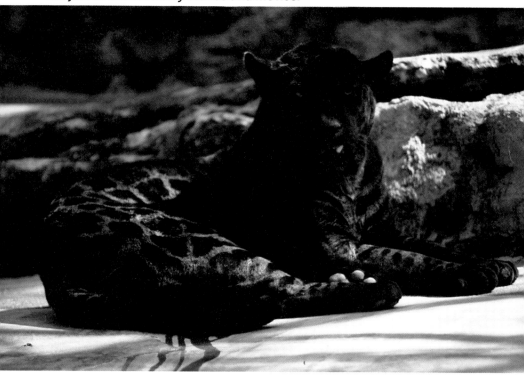

CHAPTER SIX:

Children in the 1890s enjoyed *The Jungle Book* and *The Second Jungle Book*, two animal stories. Though their style is old-fashioned, these classics by Rudyard Kipling are still read and enjoyed today.

Many of *The Jungle Book* stories are set in central India. The main character is a boy who strays from his village as a toddler. A pack of wolves finds him and adopts him. The boy, Mowgli, spends his childhood with the animals of the forest. Baloo the bear and Bagheera the black panther become his best friends and teachers. Bagheera instructs the boy in important laws of the wild.

Over time, Bagheera teaches Mowgli hunting and tree-climbing skills. He shows Mowgli how to avoid traps set by humans. The black panther takes pride in his smart pupil and spoils him. Bagheera is a star in this classic book and the popular 1967 Walt Disney movie based on the story.

An almost real storybook

In 1875 in central Asia, an eight-year-old boy was rescued from a wolf den. The boy had been raised by the wolves. He howled and would only eat raw meat.

Rudyard Kipling knew of this event. It is possible that he based *The Jungle Book* on this true tale.

Much of *The Jungle Book* is based on fact. The author gave the animals a few human traits, but mostly he kept their beastly natures and wild ways.

This is true of Bagheera, the black panther, as well. A real black panther would not feel tenderness. It would not care for humans. But a real black panther would fear a pack of baboons. It would leap over a wide stream. It would also break out of a cage and escape.

Bagheera does all of this in *The Jungle Book*. Beyond Bagheera's few human traits, Kipling gave children a real black panther to read about.

Cunning and bold

None of the jungle animals cared to cross the inky-black panther's path. He was cunning as a jackal. He was bold as a wild buffalo. He was reckless as a wounded elephant.

This is how Kipling describes Bagheera in the first chapter of *The Jungle Book*.

Someone who has a cunning nature is clever at fooling others. He or she is tricky and sly. In *The Second Jungle Book*, Bagheera performs a sly deed. Mowgli tries to protect his one human friend, Messua, from a mob of angry

Like its leopard cousins, this young jaguar will grow up to be a fierce and clever hunter.

village folk. The mob breaks down Messua's door. Their torchlight shines into the hut. Lying on the bed is Bagheera. He yawns widely to show his terrible teeth. The villagers scream and run away. Bagheera's tricky nature saves the day!

Real spotted leopards, black and fair, appear to be cunning, too. A man once saw a spotted leopard outsmart a camel. The big cat rolled on the ground near the hump-backed beast. The cat knew the camel was curious. The camel drew close to inspect this funny creature rolling on the ground. When the camel lowered its head for a look, the spotted leopard grabbed its throat. This tricky cat enjoyed a camel-meat lunch.

Bagheera is a bold cat, too. He is brave and takes risks. Bagheera, like Mowgli, was born among humans. He was kept in a cage at a king's palace. Tired of living behind bars, Bagheera escaped. In a bold move, he broke the lock with one blow of his paw and ran away.

Real spotted leopards, black and fair, are very bold. There are countless true tales of their daring natures. In Africa, a man sat eating supper in his house. A spotted leopard leaped through the open door. It skidded across the smooth floor. The cat snatched a small dog and ran back outside. This all happened in a flash. The man did not even have time to get out of his chair!

Reckless as a wounded elephant?

Kipling also describes Bagheera as reckless. Reckless means careless. Bagheera does not often behave carelessly in the jungle stories. He, like real black panthers, is cautious by nature. A real black panther, if alarmed, may kill many sheep at one time. An injured or sick black panther may kill a human. But reckless acts like these are rare. A normal, healthy black panther, like all spotted leopards, kills only enough game to survive.

Perhaps it is humans who have been reckless. Over time, humans have killed members of this species for adventure and fashion. Imagine if they do not stop. Will the only spotted leopards left be in pictures and movies?

Today, the world knows that the spotted leopard, black and fair, is endangered. The prince of cats is a wild species that must be protected.

AMBUSH 16—*A hiding place where a creature lies in wait to attack its prey by surprise.*

CAMOUFLAGE 4, 39—*An appearance that hides an animal from its enemies and prey by making it look like its natural surroundings.*

CARCASS 19, 22—*The dead body of an animal.*

CARNIVORE 21—*An animal that eats meat.*

DOMINANT GENE 8—*The gene that passes on a trait from a parent to a child, no matter what other kind of gene it is paired with.*

ENDANGERED 22, 34, 35, 38, 46—*Threatened or in danger of extinction.*

GENES 7, 8—*Tiny parts of matter in animal cells that determine the traits parents pass on to children.*

HEREDITY 6, 9—*The transfer of traits from one generation to the next.*

LITTER 5, 9, 27, 39—*The babies born from one pregnancy.*

MAN-EATER 21, 22, 35—*An animal that eats the flesh of humans.*

MELANISTIC 6, 39—*Characterized by a darkness of the skin, hair, or eyes resulting from a high level of pigment.*

NATURALIST 5—*A person who studies nature, especially plant and animal life.*

NOCTURNAL 14—*Active during the night instead of during the day.*

PARASITES 22—*Plants or animals that live on or inside larger plants or animals.*

PHASE 5, 9—*A trait or appearance that distinguishes some individuals of a group.*

PIGMENT 6—*A natural coloring material in plants and animals.*

POACHERS 38—*People who hunt or fish illegally.*

PREDATORS 27—*Animals that hunt other animals for food.*

PREY 14, 15, 16, 18, 19, 21, 27, 41—*An animal that is hunted for food by other animals.*

RAIN FOREST 4, 9—*A dense forest that has a yearly rainfall of at least 100 inches.*

RANGE 9, 25, 31, 40—*A large, open area of land.*

ROSETTES 12, 13—*The five small, dark spots on a panther's coat that form a circle. Each of these circles looks much like the paw print of an animal.*

SCAVENGER 22—*An animal that feeds on the remains of dead animals.*

SPECIES 5, 6, 10, 11, 13, 14, 19, 22, 25, 27, 34, 36, 38, 46—*A group of plants or animals with common features that set it apart from other groups.*

47